EVERYTHING SUPER BOWL

THE SUPER BOWL'S GREATEST PLAYS

BY SHANE FREDERICK

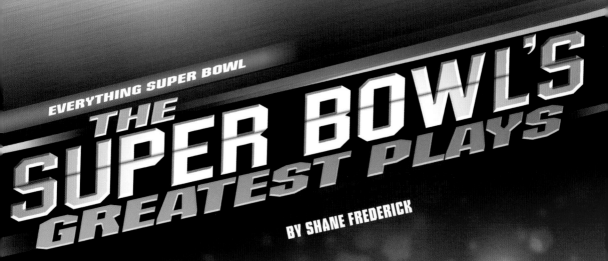

CAPSTONE PRESS
a capstone imprint

Sports Illustrated Kids Everything Super Bowl is published by
Capstone Press, 1710 Roe Crest Drive, North Mankato, Minnesota 56003
www.mycapstone.com

Library of Congress Cataloging-in-Publication Data is available on the Library of
Congress website.

ISBN 978-1-5157-2633-3 (library hardcover)
ISBN 978-1-5157-2637-1 (eBook PDF)

Editorial Credits
Nick Healy, editor; Ted Williams, designer; Eric Gohl, media researcher;
Gene Bentdahl, production specialist

Photo Credits
AP Photo: 6, Rusty Kennedy, 13; Getty Images: Bettmann, 11, Focus on Sport, 14,
Kevin Reece, 18, Rob Brown, 10; Newscom: EPA/Larry W. Smith, 28, Icon SMI/
Sporting News, 16, Icon Sportswire/Rich Graessle, 4–5; Sports Illustrated: Al
Tielemans, 22, 23, Andy Hayt, 8, 9, Damian Strohmeyer, cover (top right), 26, John
Biever, cover (top left), 20, John Iacono, 12, 15, 17, 19, John W. McDonough, cover
(bottom), 24, 29, Peter Read Miller, 21, 25, Walter Iooss Jr., 7
Design Elements: Shutterstock

Printed in the United States of America.
009677F16

TABLE OF CONTENTS

SUPER PLAYS

Early in Super Bowl 50, Denver Broncos linebacker Von Miller blew by a blocker, hit Carolina Panthers quarterback Cam Newton, and ripped the ball out of his hands. The ball rolled to the end zone, where one of Miller's teammates pounced on it for a touchdown. Miller made all kinds of big plays that day as he led the Broncos to a 24-10 victory. Perhaps none was bigger than that memorable sack and strip of the talented Newton.

Big plays such as Miller's happen in almost every Super Bowl. They are the moments that can make the difference between winning the championship and walking off the field as the other team celebrates.

The biggest plays on football's biggest stage feature perfect throws, acrobatic catches, and record-setting runs. They include surprise interceptions, forced fumbles, and game-saving tackles. Some result from errant passes, dropped balls, and missed field goals. Fans remember these amazing Super Bowl plays for years after the games are played.

◄ Von Miller

SWANN DIVE

Lynn Swann ▶

— THE FIRST BIG PLAY —

The first touchdown in Super Bowl history was a one-handed, behind-the-back grab. Green Bay Packers receiver Max McGee caught the pass from quarterback Bart Starr. The Packers won Super Bowl I over the Kansas City Chiefs by a score of 35–10.

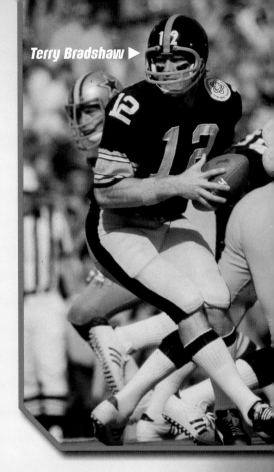

Terry Bradshaw ▶

During his career with the Pittsburgh Steelers, wide receiver Lynn Swann was known for making difficult catches look easy. His abilities were aided, he said, by his study of dance, including ballet. Swann never looked as graceful as he did in Super Bowl X, when he made one of the great catches in the history of the big game.

Quarterback Terry Bradshaw heaved a pass out of his own end zone to midfield, where Dallas Cowboys cornerback Mark Washington had Swann covered. Swann jumped high to make the catch, but the ball glanced off of his hands. As the receiver and defender tangled and fell toward the turf, Swann kept his concentration on the ball. He dived forward and hauled it in for a 53-yard gain.

Earlier in the game, Swann had twisted his body in the air to get inside Washington for an impressive catch along the sidelines. He caught just four passes that day but gained 161 yards, including a 64-yard touchdown reception. Swann helped the Steelers win 21-17 and was named the game's most valuable player (MVP).

DIESEL FUEL

John Riggins ▶

— THE FRIDGE SCORES

In 1985 the Chicago Bears sometimes lined up 335-pound defensive lineman William "The Refrigerator" Perry as a short-yardage running back. In Super Bowl XX the Fridge blasted his way into the end zone, scoring on a one-yard run. The Bears won 46-10 over the New England Patriots

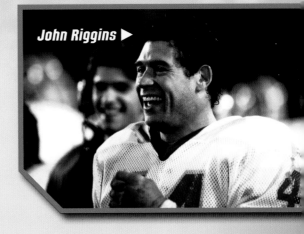

John Riggins was known as "The Diesel" because of his powerful, machine-like running style. When the playoffs following the 1982 season began, the Washington Redskins running back told coach Joe Gibbs that he wanted the ball. Gibbs made sure The Diesel got it. In Super Bowl XVII against the Miami Dolphins, Riggins ran the ball a record 38 times.

With about 10 minutes to play in the game, Washington trailed 17-13 and faced fourth down and one yard to go from the Miami 43. Field goal? Too far. Punt? No way. Not with The Diesel and a huge offensive line nicknamed "The Hogs."

Riggins took the handoff and easily gained the first down, but that wasn't all. Dolphins defensive back Don McNeal had a chance to tackle the big back for a short gain, but Riggins swatted him away like a mosquito. From there, Riggins rumbled the rest of the way to the end zone and scored the go-ahead touchdown. Washington eventually won 27-17, getting its first Super Bowl championship. Riggins rushed for 166 yards, also a record at the time, and was the game's MVP.

THE LONG RUN

Marcus Allen ▶

▲ **Marcus Allen and the Lombardi Trophy**

The Los Angeles Raiders had a commanding 28-9 lead over the Washington Redskins in Super Bowl XVIII. Raiders running back Marcus Allen was a big reason why. As the end of the third quarter neared, he had carried the ball 16 times for 72 yards and a touchdown.

Trying to get back into the game, Washington drove down to the Raiders' 26-yard line. But the Redskins got stuffed on fourth down and turned the ball back to the Raiders. That's when Allen ensured that his team would be holding up the Lombardi Trophy at the end of the game.

Taking the handoff from quarterback Jim Plunkett, Allen dashed to his left. No hole opened for him, so he turned around and reversed course. Allen broke one tackle, saw daylight in the middle of the line, and sprinted through it. He didn't stop until he crossed the goal line 74 yards down field.

"I ended up where I wanted to end up," Allen said. The Super Bowl MVP finished the game with 191 yards, a record at the time.

— PARKER PASSES ALLEN —

Marcus Allen's record 74-yard touchdown run was surpassed 22 years later. The Pittsburgh Steelers' Willie Parker sprinted 75 yards for a score in a victory over the Seattle Seahawks in Super Bowl XL.

TAYLOR-MADE TOUCHDOWN

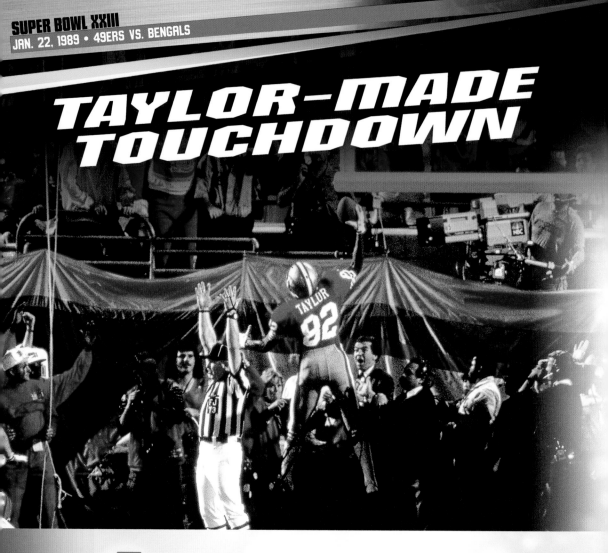

Quarterback Joe Montana was the conductor of the San Francisco 49ers' late drive to win Super Bowl XXIII. His favorite target, wide receiver Jerry Rice, was the game's MVP. Receiver John Taylor caught only one pass in that 20-16 victory over the Cincinnati Bengals. Taylor's catch, though, was the most important play of the game.

— RICE SETS THE RECORD —

Jerry Rice, the NFL's all-time leading receiver and touchdown scorer, had 11 catches for 215 yards and a touchdown in Super Bowl XXIII. His yardage total remains a Super Bowl record.

The 49ers trailed 16-13 with 3:10 remaining in the game and had to go 92 yards if they were going to score. Montana, who was already a two-time Super Bowl MVP, was cool as usual. He tossed three passes to receiver Jerry Rice for 51 yards and three to running back Roger Craig for 29 more. An 8-yard pass to Craig moved the 49ers to the Bengals' 10-yard line with 39 seconds left on the clock.

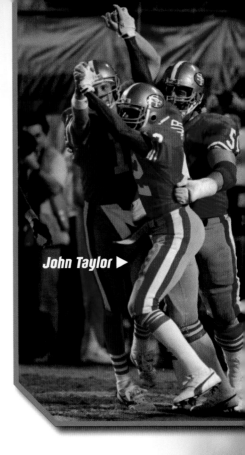

John Taylor ▶

Rice was a decoy on the next play, and Craig was the intended receiver. But Craig was covered. Taylor split the safeties and drifted to the back of the end zone. There wasn't a big window to throw into, but Montana delivered a perfect strike into Taylor's hands. Taylor's touchdown capped the thrilling, come-from-behind win.

— STICK TO KICKING —

One of the worst plays in Super Bowl history took place in Super Bowl VII. Miami Dolphins kicker Garo Yepremian tried to throw a pass after his field goal try was blocked. The ball slipped out of his hand. Then he tipped the ball in the air. An opponent grabbed it and ran for a touchdown. Fortunately for Yepremian, the Dolphins still won.

WIDE RIGHT

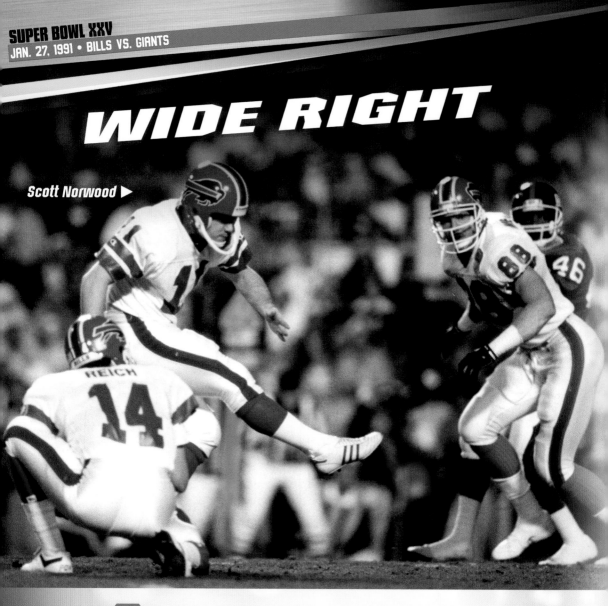

Scott Norwood ▶

Only one team in NFL history has played in four consecutive Super Bowls: the Buffalo Bills. Sadly for Bills fans, their team never won.

— CLUTCH KICKERS —

Three last-second kicks have won Super Bowls. The New England Patriots' Adam Vinatieri booted two—in Super Bowl XXXVI against the St. Louis Rams and XXXVIII against the Carolina Panthers. The Baltimore Colts' Jim O'Brien kicked a winner in Super Bowl V against the Dallas Cowboys.

Their best chance came in their first appearance, Super Bowl XXV against the New York Giants. Trailing 20-19 with 2:16 remaining in the game, the Bills started a desperation drive on their own 10-yard line. They needed to get into field goal range for kicker Scott Norwood, whose longest kick of that season was 48 yards.

Quarterback Jim Kelly led his team to the 30-yard line with eight seconds left on the clock. Earlier in the game, Norwood had connected from 23 yards out. Now he was trying a 47-yarder for a championship. The snap and the hold were good, and Norwood's kick had the distance. But the ball never hooked in toward the uprights and sailed just a few feet wide to the right. The Giants celebrated their narrow victory.

— STAR-SPANGLED SINGER

Pop singer Whitney Houston set the standard for performances of "The Star Spangled Banner" when she sang before Super Bowl XXV in 1991. The game was played 10 days after the start of the first Gulf War, and a patriotic Tampa Stadium crowd of 73,813 cheered wildly after her powerful performance.

MOST VALUABLE RETURNER

Desmond Howard was a great college football player, winning the Heisman Trophy at the University of Michigan. But he struggled in his first four seasons as a professional. In 1996 he was one of the last players to make the cut for the Green Bay Packers, his third NFL team. Instead of vying for a starting wide-receiver spot, however, he was asked to return punts and kicks. It was a job at which he excelled.

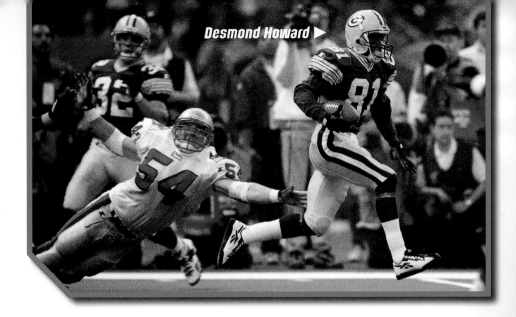

Desmond Howard ▶

Following that season, the Packers met the New England Patriots in Super Bowl XXXI. The Packers led 27-14 at halftime, thanks in part to some big punt returns by Howard. His returns had given his offense a short field, and the Packers had cashed in.

Late in the third quarter, the Patriots finally got some momentum. They pulled to within six points after a Curtis Martin touchdown. But Howard made sure the Pats' momentum didn't last long.

He caught the ensuing kickoff on the 1-yard line and sprinted ahead. He broke one tackle, got a key block from receiver Don Beebe, and watched as the field parted in front of him. His 99-yard return for a touchdown, plus a two-point conversion, gave Green Bay a two-touchdown lead. Howard became a surprising Super Bowl MVP.

— WHAT A START! —

Super Bowl XLI began with a 92-yard kickoff return for a touchdown by the Chicago Bears' Devin Hester. But things went downhill for the Bears. They ended up losing 29-17 to Peyton Manning's Indianapolis Colts.

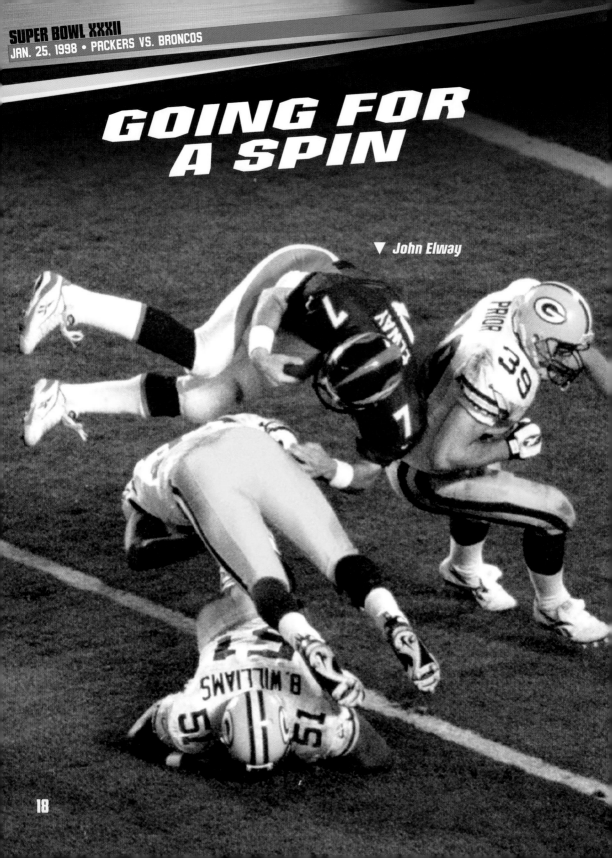

GOING FOR A SPIN

▼ John Elway

In the prime of his career, quarterback John Elway went to three Super Bowls in a span of four years. But he and the Denver Broncos got blown out each time. It took eight years after that third devastating loss for Elway to finally return to the big game.

Many people didn't give the 37-year-old and his Broncos a chance in Super Bowl XXXII. They faced the defending-champion Green Bay Packers and their own gun-slinging quarterback, Brett Favre. But the Broncos weren't going to get blown out this time.

With the game tied 17-17 late in the third quarter, Elway put his aging body on the line. On the run after a third-down pass play had broken down, Elway saw three defenders bearing down on him. He knew he had to dive forward for the first down. As he left his feet, he got drilled by All-Pro safety LeRoy Butler and then again by linebacker Brian Williams. Elway's body spun in midair like the blades of a helicopter. When he hit the ground, he had the first down.

Inspired by their leader's effort, the Broncos took the lead two plays later and never gave it up. Elway finally had his championship.

— OUT ON TOP —

John Elway won a second Super Bowl the season after winning his first. He was the MVP in a 34-19 win over the Atlanta Falcons, throwing one touchdown pass and running for another. It was Elway's final NFL game.

TITANIC TACKLE

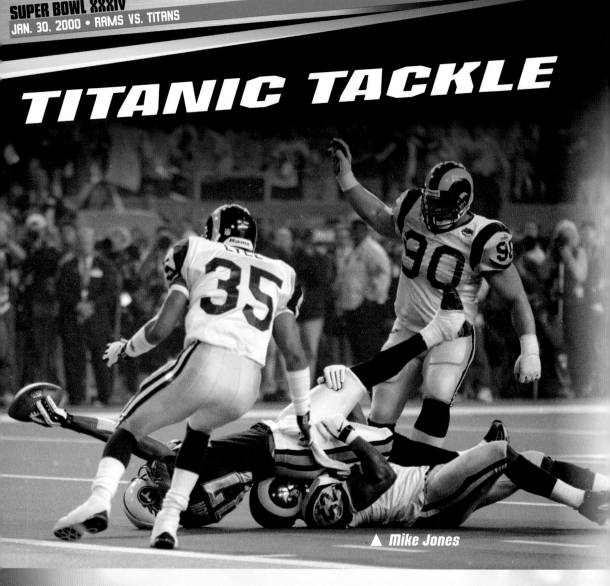

▲ Mike Jones

In 1999 the St. Louis Rams were known as the "Greatest Show on Turf." With quarterback Kurt Warner, running back Marshall Faulk, and receivers Isaac Bruce and Torry Holt, the team ranked among the best offenses in NFL history. Winning Super Bowl XXXIV, though, came down to defense.

With six seconds remaining in the fourth quarter, the Tennessee Titans trailed 23-16. But the Titans had the ball on the Rams' 10-yard line. If they could score a touchdown on the final play of regulation time (and kick the extra point), they would force overtime.

Wide receiver Kevin Dyson ran a slant pattern and caught a pass from quarterback Steve McNair at the 4-yard line. Dyson lunged for the goal line but was stopped in his tracks by Rams linebacker Mike Jones. Jones wrapped his arms around Dyson's legs, then twisted, turned, and pulled Dyson toward the turf. The receiver stretched out with the ball, straining toward the goal line. But as Dyson hit the turf, the ball was one yard short. Jones' tackle was a Super Bowl-winner for the Rams.

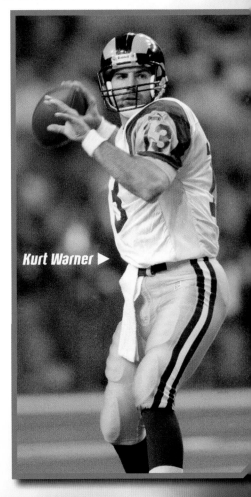

Kurt Warner ▶

TIPTOE TO A TITLE

◄ Santonio Holmes

— RECEIVERS OF STEEL —

Six wide receivers have earned Super Bowl MVP honors. Three of them have been Steelers: Santonio Holmes, Hines Ward, and Lynn Swann.

Super Bowl XLIII already had one play that would go down in NFL history. In the last seconds of the first half, Pittsburgh Steelers linebacker James Harrison intercepted Arizona Cardinals quarterback Kurt Warner at the goal line. Then the huge defender rumbled 100 yards the other way for a touchdown that gave his team a 17-7 lead.

The Cardinals came back strong in the second half. With 2:37 remaining in the fourth quarter, they led 23-20. That was plenty of time for quarterback Ben Roethlisberger and his collection of talented receivers. Third-year wideout Santonio Holmes was the main target that day.

Holmes had three of his nine catches on the final drive, including one to get the Steelers to the 6-yard line with 49 seconds to go. Two plays later, Roethlisberger tossed another ball to Holmes. This one was a high pass to the back corner of the end zone. The athletic Holmes reached high and snatched the ball. As he fell to the ground, he tapped the toes of both feet in bounds. He had the winning score—and one of football's most famous catches.

ONSIDE AMBUSH

The New Orleans Saints trailed the Indianapolis Colts 10-6 at halftime of Super Bowl XLIV. The Colts, with superstar quarterback Peyton Manning leading the offense, were set to get the ball to start the second half. Saints coach Sean Payton decided he didn't want that to happen. He decided to make one of the gutsiest calls in Super Bowl history.

◀ *Chris Reis*

— HAVE YOUR PICK —

Oakland Raiders linebacker Rod Martin set a Super Bowl record with three interceptions, all off Philadelphia Eagles quarterback Ron Jaworski. The Raiders won Super Bowl XV 27-10.

Payton told his team it was going to start the second half with an "ambush." He called an onside kick in hopes to give the ball to his own star quarterback, Drew Brees, right away. The gamble worked.

Thomas Morstead's kick rolled on the turf and bounced off the chest of a Colts player. Then Saints safety Chris Reis fell on it and held on as several other players piled on.

Brees led a touchdown charge after the surprise attack, and the Saints took the lead and the momentum. New Orleans' 31-17 victory was sealed by another memorable play. Defensive back Tracy Porter made a 74-yard interception return for a touchdown on a Manning pass late in the game.

◀ *Tracy Porter*

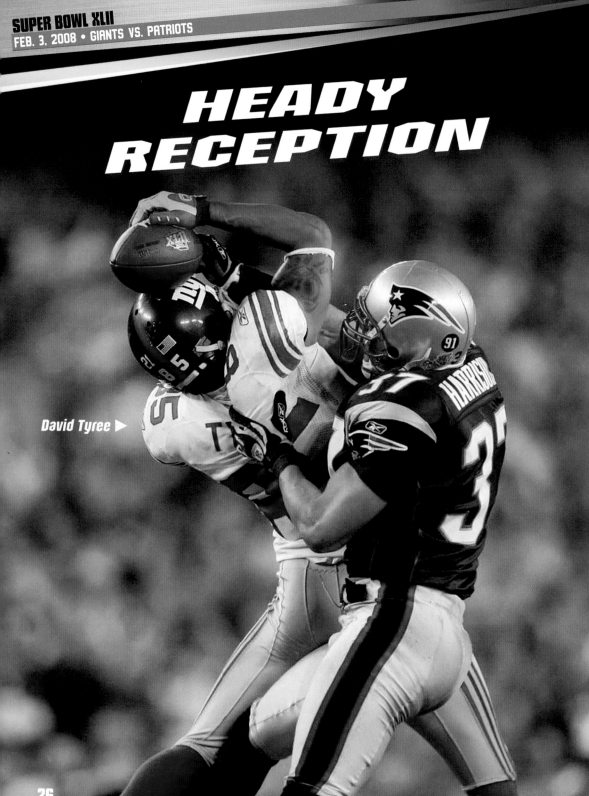

HEADY RECEPTION

David Tyree ▶

It was desperation time. The New York Giants were driving to win Super Bowl XLII and prevent history from happening. Their opponent, the New England Patriots, were looking to stay undefeated after going 16-0 in the regular season and winning two playoff games.

The Giants faced third down with 5 yards to go on their own 44-yard line. There was only 1:15 left in the game. Patriots defensive end Jarvis Green had quarterback Eli Manning in his grasp for a sure sack. Somehow Manning escaped Green's clutches and heaved the ball 40 yards through the air.

Receiver David Tyree jumped and reached as high as he could to catch the ball. As he fell to the turf, Tyree pinned the ball to his helmet with one hand, doing whatever he could to keep it from falling incomplete. Defensive back Rodney Harrison hit Tyree and tried to swat away the ball. Tyree held on.

Four plays later Manning tossed the go-ahead touchdown to Plaxico Burress. The Giants took the lead and kept it. The helmet catch was the game's key play—and the last NFL catch Tyree ever made. After that season he failed to catch on with the Patriots or another NFL team.

— A PERFECT SEASON —

The 1972 Miami Dolphins remain the last team to go undefeated through the Super Bowl. They went 14-0 in the regular season and won three playoff games, including Super Bowl VII over the Washington Redskins.

BUTLER DID IT

◄ Malcolm Butler

28

Super Bowl XLIX came down to one play and one yard. The Seattle Seahawks were at the New England Patriots' 1-yard line, trailing 28-24 with 26 seconds to go in the game. Move the ball three feet, and Seattle would repeat as champions. Get stuffed, and New England would win its fourth title in 14 years, but its first in a decade.

The Seahawks had bruising running back Marshawn Lynch on the team. Lynch, who was known as "Beast Mode," already had 102 yards rushing and a touchdown in the game. Seattle, however, opted to have star quarterback Russell Wilson drop back to pass. The call was to throw a quick slant to receiver Ricardo Lockette.

Patriots cornerback Malcolm Butler scanned the field before the ball was snapped and read the play perfectly. In full sprint, Butler jumped in front of Lockette at the last possible moment. He intercepted the pass as he crashed into the receiver on the goal line. In a game full of superstars such as Wilson, Lynch, and Patriots quarterback Tom Brady, Butler became the unlikely hero.

— STAY TUNED —

Almost everything stops for the Super Bowl, it seems, because almost everybody is watching. There were 70,288 people inside University of Phoenix stadium for the Super Bowl between the Patriots and Seahawks. Another 114.4 million people were watching on TV—in the United States alone! That made it the most-watched television broadcast in U.S. history.

GLOSSARY

ambush—a surprise attack

broadcast—to send out a television or radio program

conductor—a leader who directs a kind of performance

consecutive—following each other without interruption

decoy—a person or thing that leads another person into danger or a trap

desperation—having little hope of success

diesel—a vehicle such a truck or bus that uses diesel fuel

ensured—made certain or safe

momentum—strength or force to continue moving forward or grow stronger

onside kick—a short kickoff that gives the kicking team a chance to recover the ball

reception—in football, a catch of a forward pass

vying—competing against another player or team

READ MORE

Braun, Eric. *Super Bowl Records.* Everything Super Bowl. North Mankato, Minn.: Capstone Press, 2017.

Editors of Sports Illustrated. *Sports Illustrated Super Bowl Gold: 50 Years of the Big Game.* New York: Sports Illustrated Books, an imprint of Time Inc. Books, 2015.

Hetrick, Hans. *Six Degrees of Peyton Manning: Connecting Football Stars.* Six Degrees of Sports. North Mankato, Minn.: Capstone Press, 2015.

INTERNET SITES

FactHound offers a safe, fun way to find Internet sites related to this book. All of the sites have been researched by our staff.

Here's all you do:

Visit www.facthound.com

Type in this code: 9781515726333

 **Super-cool stuff!** Check out projects, games and lots more at **www.capstonekids.com**

INDEX